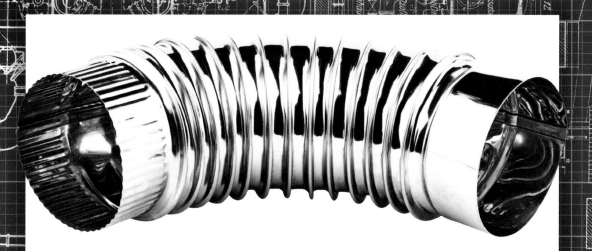

SKILLED TRADE CAREERS
HVAC TECHS

by Gary Sprott

Rourke
Educational Media

A Division of
Carson Dellosa Education

Before Reading: *Building Background Knowledge and Vocabulary*

Building background knowledge can help children process new information and build upon what they already know. Before reading a book, it is important to tap into what children already know about the topic. This will help them develop their vocabulary and increase their reading comprehension.

Questions and Activities to Build Background Knowledge:

1. Look at the front cover of the book and read the title. What do you think this book will be about?
2. What do you already know about this topic?
3. Take a book walk and skim the pages. Look at the table of contents, photographs, captions, and bold words. Did these text features give you any information or predictions about what you will read in this book?

Vocabulary: *Vocabulary Is Key to Reading Comprehension*

Use the following directions to prompt a conversation about each word.

- Read the vocabulary words.
- What comes to mind when you see each word?
- What do you think each word means?

Vocabulary Words:
- ducts
- efficiency
- nonrenewable
- radiator
- ventilation
- vocational

During Reading: *Reading for Meaning and Understanding*

To achieve deep comprehension of a book, children are encouraged to use close reading strategies. During reading, it is important to have children stop and make connections. These connections result in deeper analysis and understanding of a book.

Close Reading a Text

During reading, have children stop and talk about the following:

- Any confusing parts
- Any unknown words
- Text to text, text to self, text to world connections
- The main idea in each chapter or heading

Encourage children to use context clues to determine the meaning of any unknown words. These strategies will help children learn to analyze the text more thoroughly as they read.

When you are finished reading this book, turn to the next-to-last page for After Reading Questions and an Activity.

TABLE OF CONTENTS

ON THE JOB

Imagine living in steamy Louisiana without air conditioning. Or snowy Montana without heat. High-tech cooling units and furnaces make it possible for us to control the temperature wherever we live. Not too hot. Not too cold. Hey, just like Goldilocks!

HVAC techs are the professionals who know all about these systems. We can thank them for being comfortable year-round.

A Red-Hot Job Market!

There are about 370,000 HVAC techs in the United States. That number is rising faster than the temperature in Arizona in July! The push to use less energy and lower pollution means more jobs for techs.

HVAC techs install and maintain heating, **ventilation**, and air conditioning systems in homes, schools, businesses, and other buildings. They inspect and repair broken equipment and replace old parts. HVAC techs help control air quality and temperature. This lets people study, work, and shop in comfortable and safe environments.

ventilation (ven-tuh-LAY-shuhn): the process of bringing fresh air in and pushing stale air out

HVAC techs use different ways to heat buildings. Some heaters burn oil or gas. Others warm water for a **radiator**.

HVAC techs also know how to cool things off. Refrigeration keeps food fresh as it travels from a farm or warehouse to a grocery store—and then to your kitchen! Professionals who work with these systems may be called HVACR techs. The *R* is for *refrigeration*.

radiator (RAY-dee-ay-tur): a series of pipes that circulate hot water or steam to heat a room

Refrigerated trucks help keep ice cream icy until it hits your tongue!

These are ruins of a Roman hypocaust. They were also used in bath houses to keep the water hot.

People have been finding new ways to stay toasty ever since they discovered fire. The ancient Romans used a system called a hypocaust. Fires were kept burning in a basement under the building. Rising hot air warmed the floors of Roman homes. No wonder the Romans were always wearing sandals!

Chilling Out in the Sunshine State

In 1940, about two million people lived in hot, humid Florida. Today, there are nearly 22 million! What happened? Air conditioning happened! The cooling technology led to a population boom.

Heating and cooling buildings uses lots of energy. Most energy is produced by burning **nonrenewable** resources, such as coal and natural gas. But, they are not good for the planet.

HVAC techs help by installing systems that use green energy, also called renewable energy. Solar panels capture the sun's warmth. Geothermal systems tap into planet Earth itself! Water is heated or chilled as it flows through underground pipes. Down there, the temperature stays pretty steady year-round.

nonrenewable (nahn-ri-NOO-uh-buhl): difficult or impossible to replace in a short time

Solar panels like these provide energy without hurting the planet.

WHAT'S IN MY TOOLBOX?

HVAC techs use general tools such as screwdrivers, hammers, saws, and drills. But they also need some very special equipment. Leak detectors and pressure gauges pinpoint where liquids or gases are escaping from lines. Crimpers seal pipes and **ducts** so they fit together snugly.

ducts (duhkts): channels or tubular runways that carry air, liquid, or cables from one place to another

Equipment, such as these refrigerant pressure gauges, must be inspected regularly to keep it working properly.

20X25X4

Special filters keep the air clean and protect HVAC systems from damage.

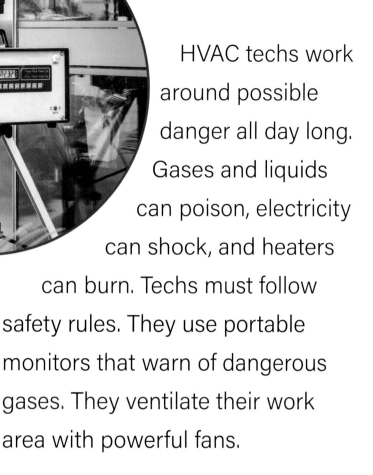

HVAC techs work around possible danger all day long. Gases and liquids can poison, electricity can shock, and heaters can burn. Techs must follow safety rules. They use portable monitors that warn of dangerous gases. They ventilate their work area with powerful fans.

Cleaner Air

Dust, dirt, and pet hair. It's tough to keep a house (or even just your room!) clean. HVAC techs install filters to catch the yucky stuff. That helps keep the air we breathe clean.

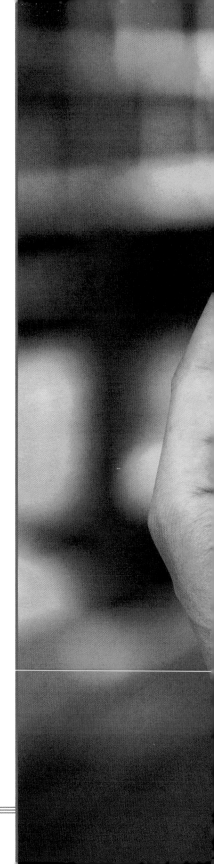

HVAC techs use sensors, wi-fi, and software to control heating, cooling, and ventilation in smart buildings. This digital technology boosts energy **efficiency** because temperatures can be controlled automatically. Want to cool down your house before you get home from the beach? No problem! Just use a smartphone to adjust the thermostat.

efficiency (i-FISH-uhn-see): working or operating well, quickly, and without waste

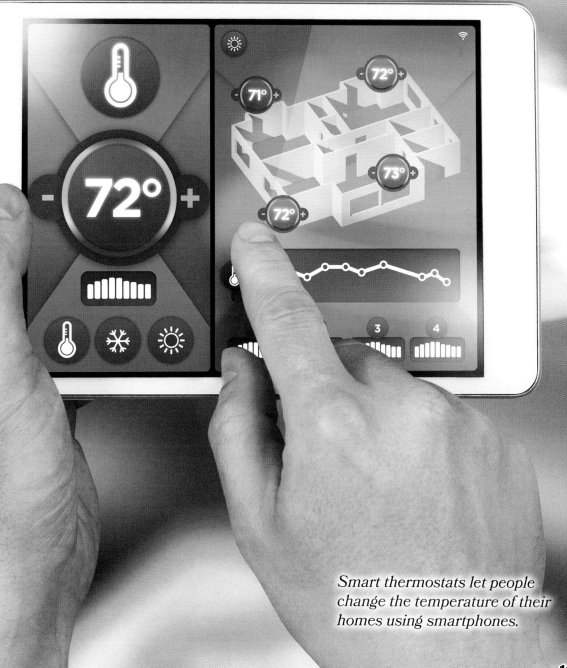

Smart thermostats let people change the temperature of their homes using smartphones.

LEARNING THE TRADE

Interested in becoming an HVAC tech? That's great! Here's a hot tip: It's cool to be in school! At least a high school diploma is required for this career.

Science (including physics) and math are important subjects to know well. And don't forget reading. Techs must understand blueprints and be able to explain instructions to customers.

Studying STEM subjects (math, technology, engineering, and math) forms a good foundation for skilled trade careers.

Many employers prefer to hire HVAC techs who have earned an associate's degree or certification from a vocational school.

Many students attend **vocational** colleges to build skills for this trade. They study how liquids and gases are heated and cooled. They learn how air circulates around a room or building. They practice connecting ducts so that they're air-tight and don't waste energy.

vocational (voh-KAY-shuh-nuhl): relating to a job, profession, or occupation

Hands-On and Online!

Many schools offer training in the classroom and online. Some students already have a job. Doing schoolwork on a smartphone or computer means they don't have to miss too many days of work.

After college, it's time to become an apprentice. Apprentices work alongside experienced technicians who are there to answer questions. Apprentices start with simpler projects. Then, they tackle trickier tasks.

Apprenticeship programs can last five years. They are offered by workers' groups such as unions, as well as by companies that make HVAC systems.

HVAC techs can work for large companies or start their own businesses.

HVAC techs need special training to do some types of work. Liquids and gases used in refrigerators and air conditioners can damage Earth's atmosphere.

In the U.S., techs must pass a test to prove they can safely handle these substances, known as coolants. Techs who complete training programs and earn certifications are in demand for high-paying jobs.

New technology and awareness about global warming are quickly changing this skilled trade career. HVAC techs must be lifelong learners to stay ahead in their profession. Organizations, such as the National Center for Construction Education and Research (NCCER), offer training programs for HVAC techs.

A Big Room to Cool!

Thousands of people attend the Air-Conditioning, Heating, and Refrigeration Expo each year. They learn about new heating and cooling products and attend training sessions with experts. The conference is 90 years old and is the world's biggest HVAC event.

DUCT

armacell

MEMORY GAME

Look at the pictures. What do you remember reading on the pages where each image appeared?

INDEX

AFTER READING QUESTIONS

1. How many HVAC techs are there in the U.S.?

2. How did people heat their homes in ancient Rome?

3. How does a geothermal system work?

4. Why would an HVAC tech use crimpers?

5. What subjects are important to study for HVAC techs?

ACTIVITY

Investigate the heating and cooling systems in your home. What equipment do they use? What pipes and ducts run to and from the equipment? Ask a parent to help you research. Then, with permission, experiment with the thermostat. What happens to the equipment when you turn the thermostat up? What happens when you turn it down? Don't forget to return the thermostat to its original setting.

ABOUT THE AUTHOR

Gary Sprott is a writer in Tampa, Florida. He has written books about ancient cultures, plants, animals, and automobiles. Gary had to buy a new air conditioner for his house. It was very expensive. But he thinks it was worth every penny. Did we mention Gary lives in Florida?

www.rourkeeducationalmedia.com

PHOTO CREDITS: page 1: ©OlekStock / iStockphoto.com; page 1: ©xresch / Pixabay; page 3: ©Bet_Noire / iStockphoto.com; page 5: ©sturti / iStockphoto.com; page 6: ©fstop123 / iStockphoto.com; page 9: ©Andrei Stanescu / iStockphoto.com; page 10: ©StockPhotosArt / iStockphoto.com; page 13: ©Cindy Shebley / iStockphoto.com; page 15: ©nikom1234 / iStockphoto.com; page 16: ©Charles Knowles / shutterstock.com; page 17: ©silkwayrain / iStockphoto.com; page 19: ©Maxiphoto / iStockphoto.com; page 21: ©SDI Productions / iStockphoto.com; page 22: ©fizkes / iStockphoto.com; page 25: ©sturti / iStockphoto.com; page 26: ©dima_sidelnikov / iStockphoto.com; page 29: ©Hardcast / Flickr

Edited by: Madison Capitano
Cover design by: Rhea Magaro-Wallace
Interior design by: Book Buddy Media

Library of Congress PCN Data

HVAC Techs / Gary Sprott
(Skilled Trade Careers)
ISBN 978-173163-834-2 (hard cover)
ISBN 978-1-73163-911-0 (soft cover)
ISBN 978-1-73163-988-2 (e-Book)
ISBN 978-1-73164-065-9 (e-Pub)
Library of Congress Control Number: 2020930212

Rourke Educational Media
Printed in the United States of America
01-1942011937